THIS YEARBOOK BELONGS TO...

....

LOVE YOU GUYS!

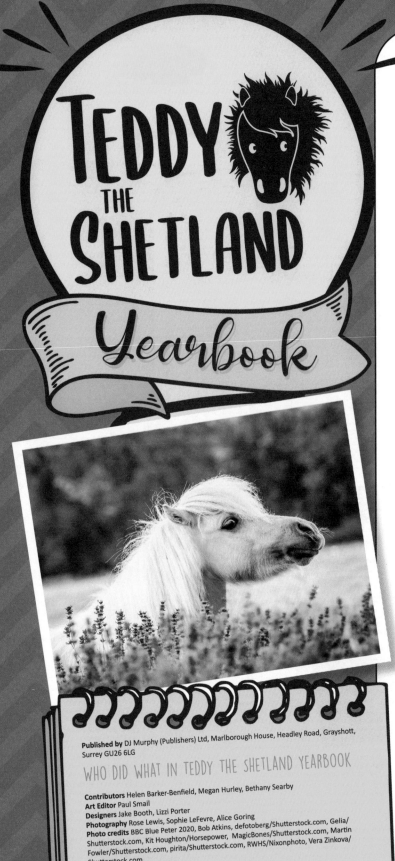

TEDDY THE SHETLAND Yearbook

Published by DJ Murphy (Publishers) Ltd, Marlborough House, Headley Road, Grayshott, Surrey GU26 6LG

WHO DID WHAT IN TEDDY THE SHETLAND YEARBOOK

Contributors Helen Barker-Benfield, Megan Hurley, Bethany Searby
Art Editor Paul Smail
Designers Jake Booth, Lizzi Porter
Photography Rose Lewis, Sophie LeFevre, Alice Goring
Photo credits BBC Blue Peter 2020, Bob Atkins, defotoberg/Shutterstock.com, Gelia/Shutterstock.com, Kit Houghton/Horsepower, MagicBones/Shutterstock.com, Martin Fowler/Shutterstock.com, pirita/Shutterstock.com, RWHS/Nixonphoto, Vera Zinkova/Shutterstock.com
Publishing Director Zoe Cannon
Commercial Director Abigail Cannon
Managing Director Kate Austin

Teddy the Shetland Yearbook is produced under license by DJ Murphy (Publishers) Ltd. © Copyright DJ Murphy (Publishers) Ltd. Printed by Graphicom via dell'Industria – 36100 Vicenza, Italy. ISBN 978-1-913787-01-1

MEET AND GREET

All about me

Name: Teddy
Born: 2015
Breed: Miniature Shetland Pony
Family: Alice and Molly are the hoomans, Finley and Theo are my horsey bros, then there's Rusty the working Cocker, Rocky the curly Cavachon and Chip the Spaniel

Loves: Snax, my fans and da cute children I visit in my day job as a therapy pony
Dislikes: Mud – I hate getting dirty and you won't often see me roll
Find me on: Instagram @Teddytheshetland #InternationalHeartbreaker, #floofking #snaxplz Facebook and YouTube teddytheshetland

HELLO MR DUDE, SIR!

The long and short of it!

TEDDY STANDS A PROUD 78CM TALL, BUT HOW DOES THAT STACK UP?

- World-famous Dressage horse Valegro is 16 hands, which is a whopping 162cm

- A showjumping obstacle is anything up to 1.6 metres high, which is 160cm

- This Esme is 168cm tall

- An average three-step mounting block is 60cm – so I've got 18cm on them!

The gd life

Teddy came to live with Alice as a young foal, with a view to him being a companion for her young event horses. Fairly quickly, he started going to events up and down the country with her top event horse Finley. It was soon clear that the bond they shared was unbreakable and that they had become besties forever.

The story of Teddy's life as an #International heartbreaker began when owner Alice's cousins suggested that she set up an Instagram account for him, so that she could share photos of her adorable new Shetland pony. Along with Alice's sister Molly, who is Teddy's ghostwriter, the trio have taken Insta and Facebook by storm.

Teddy is not just a pretty picture... he's also gaining legendary status as a therapy pony – visiting hospices and getting his fair share of kissez from both the children and staff. This has led to appearances on BBC news and even Blue Peter, where he aims to raise awareness of the good work that all therapy pets do. Often behind the scenes – these animals don't do it for fame and fortune!

Mutual respect!

♥ MY PARENTS ♥

The future

What's next for this tiny pony with big ideas? Well, Teddy would like to take his superstar status global... but with a full-time career as a scientist and being equally full-on as a serious amateur eventer, Alice may have different ideas. Watch this space!

MY BEST Side ♥

Accidental model

ME AND DORIS ♡

Hide and seek

FAST MOOVIN'

This really happened. Pinch me!

8

Shades for sunny days

Me and my ma

DOG YOGA

FOUR YEARS YOUNG

Time for a career change

MMMMMM!

If this is not a snack, don't put a carrot on it!

BACK YARD BUDDIES

FIND OUT ALL YOU NEED TO KNOW ABOUT THE REST OF MY HOUSE MATES

#EventingPro

Name: Finley
Born: 2005
Breed: Anglo Arab
Height: 15hh

Special skills: Jumping fences taller than him
Loves: Galloping with his tiny pal (a.k.a. me)
Dislikes: Going anywhere without me!

#RealLifeUnicorn

Name: Theo
Born: 2012
Breed: Thoroughbred X Welsh
Height: 15.2hh

Special skills: Doing a rocket impression over jumps
Loves: Overachieving and going on daytrips
Dislikes: Knocking jumps down

#ChunkyButFunky

Name: Podge
Born: 2019
Breed: Miniature Shetland Pony
Height: Smaller than me (for now)

Special skills: Standing on a bucket
Loves: Snax and having a laugh with me and Rusty
Dislikes: Dieting

#CheerfulChippy

Name: Chip
Born: 2016
Breed: Cocker Spaniel
Height: A bit bigger than Rusty

Special skills: Pro-cuddler
Loves: Going on long walks
Dislikes: Cats

#DaFloofMeister

Name: Rocky
Born: 2011
Breed: Curly Cavachon
Height: A bit smaller than Rusty

Special skills: Going for a spin on my back!
Loves: Dinner time and naps
Dislikes: Getting his paws wet

11

Teddy's TIMELINE

Time flies when you're having fun!

DA CUTEST FROM DAY ONE!

DOB
July 2015

← Posts

teddytheshetland

♡ ◯ ▽

Liked by 1,669 others

teddytheshetland My name is Teddy, I am a 5 month old miniature Shetland! Please follow me 🐴 ... more

View all 153 comments

MY FIRST POST
Did you see it?

December 2015

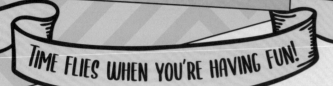

1,000 FOLLOWERS
At the start of the year we hit the big time!
#TinyHooves
#BigPlans
January 2016

10,000 FOLLOWERS
Three weeks later... another milestone.

January 2016

THE FIRST THERAPY PONY VISIT
Induction into a very exclusive club.

December 2017

WHEN DA FLOOF WENT VIRAL
Sandown Park Racecourse Christmas advert.
Adored by thousands!

December 2017

HOODIE: MODEL'S OWN

MERCH LAUNCHES
Kanye, I'm comin' for ya!

March 2020

I INTRODUCED THE BABY BROTHER
I never knew always wanted.

January 2020

♥ 100k

100,000 FOLLOWERS
I couldn't do this without
you guys by my side.
Honestly, you're the best.

August 2019

First things first, I need to make sure I look good, all the time. Exhausting, but so worth it. Da floof doesn't take care of itself, you know!

I need a good team around me. Enter Alice and Molly. While they will be the first to admit that they have the best subject matter to work with, it's important that they always show my most flattering side and that my words aren't distorted. I have to stay true to myself. I know you lovely people appreciate me being authentic!

It's good to have friends around to share the fun, but not the limelight. On my account, Rusty – however cute he is on a daily basis – has to step in line. He has his own social feed for the days when he wants to shine. But, I couldn't do this alone and I appreciate all the help my buddies give me. Always remembering to say thank you is so important!

Making your fans laugh is key – a funny face or cute look directly to the camera is always a good tactic for maximum ooooh's and ahhhh's. Breaking the internet is always my goal!

13

The Shetland FAM!

LOOKIN' GD

CHECK OUT SOME FACTS ON MY FELLOW PONIES, AREN'T WE DA CUTEST?!

TOP 10
MUST-KNOWS

1 WHAT'S THE BIG IDEA?!
We are not miniature ponies. We are fully fledged equines bred to be just under one metre tall.

2 MIND YOUR MANNERS
As a breed we are feisty, but in a good way. As well as being easy to train, we're lively and courageous, but we also have more spirit than, well Spirit...

3 SMALL PEOPLE ONLY

A child can ride a Shetland and we make the perfect first pony! A light adult would have fun riding us, too.

LITTLE HOOMANS

4 HIGH JUMP

Did you know Shetlands are good at jumping? See some of our competing exploits on page 56.

5 ON THE MAP

We really do originate from Shetland. This is a gorgeous, windswept and remote cluster of islands off the top of Scotland.

6 DA FLOOF

Other Shetland ponies may have amazingly fluffy coats, but none of them have world-famous floof like mine. FACT!

7 SO THIS SEASON DAARRLING!

We can be chestnut, black, grey, brown, bay, roan, palomino, dun, cream and chestnut coloured. One thing we are not is spotted.

SHETLAND COLOURS

8 WALK THE WALK

Some people say we have an over-pronounced trot. Watch my vids and you will see it's more like a catwalk model on the runway...

10 SOCIAL STARS

We are super-sociable. And not just on Insta or Facebook! I love meeting new people. But, just cos I am da friendliest Shetland you'll ever come across, be aware that some of my breed might be a bit more, um aloof!

ASK THEIR OWNER BEFORE YOU SNUGGLE A STRANGER SHETLAND PONY!

9 RUN LIKE THE WIND

A Shetland pony is a superfast running machine. We can reach speeds of up to 30 mph, especially if there is a reward for our efforts... Some of our kind even make great running partners for their hoomans.

30

A to Z

OF TEDDY THE SHETLAND

ALMOST EVERYTHING YOUZ NEEDS TO KNOWZ ABOUT ME!

A is for Alice
My favourite hooman in the whole world!

B is for Badminton Horse Trials
I nailed the cross-country limbo 100%.

READY, STEADY, JUMP

C is for Cheesin'
Did someone say cheese?

D is for the day job
Being a therapy pony is the bestest thing of all.

F has to be my signature FLOOF!

E is for making an entrance at all the events I go to. #GoBig!

G is for guard floof
If your name's not on the list you ain't comin' in.

H is for house pet
Sooo need my own pad!

I is for #International heartbreaker
Your words, not mine.

I THINK I'M FUNNY...

J is for joker
I just can't help myself sometimes.

K is for Kissez
Get ready for some serious snugglez.

O has to be Olympia
My most favourite day out.

P is for Pringles
Sour cream and onion, obvs!

L is for Larry and Bob
Love our Monday morning conference calls.

Q is the undisputed Queen of my heart, Doris_the_shetland.

TRUE LOVE

M is for modelling
When you look this good you've just got to flaunt it.

READY FOR MY CLOSE UP

R is for Rusty, the best baby brother this pony could ever wish for.

N is for never giving up on your dreams
If you can floof it, you can do it!

S is for Shetland, the best breed on the planet.

T is for twinning with my baby bro.

V is for videos
Check 'em out on da Insta.

U is for Unicorn
When I transform from  to 🦄

W is for workouts with the mini peoplez Kizzy and Ettie.

X is for XXL which, believe it or not, is my size in hooman clothing!

Y is for yawwwwwn!

Z is for Zzzzzzz preferably in the mothership's cozy bed.

TEDDY THE SHETLAND

crazy hair, don't care

The day job

Find out about my very important role as a therapy pony here...

DOING WHAT I DO BEST

WHAT EXACTLY IS A THERAPY PONY?

Therapy ponies are calm, quiet visitors for sick adults and children in hospital. The great thing about a Shetland pony is that we are just the right height to chat face to face with someone in a hospital bed, wheelchair or armchair. This makes it easy to give us a hug or stroke. We love the attention and we're great company! The staff enjoy us visiting, too, as they love seeing their patients' faces light up. I bet they talk about us for hours after we've gone!

PET–TASTIC
DID YOU KNOW DOGS AND CATS CAN BE THERAPY PETS, TOO.

TRAINING SESSIONS

I had to undergo rigourous training. They don't let just anyone be a therapy pony, you know! We started off with lots of walks in busy places so that my hooman could see that I was calm under pressure. They call it desensitising but I call it showing off my skills while pretending I've not noticed I've got an audience!

WHO A THERAPY PONY HELPS

We are available to help anyone who needs us. I visit lots of different people every year, but my most special memories are made visiting poorly children and putting a smile on their faces. They are small, like me, and so brave! Us therapy ponies can also work with adults, blind people, cancer patients (check out Doris on page 42) and dementia sufferers.

HOW A THERAPY PONY HELPS

A therapy pony provides a chance for patients to think of something other than their treatment.

THE DAY I VISITED
Blue Peter

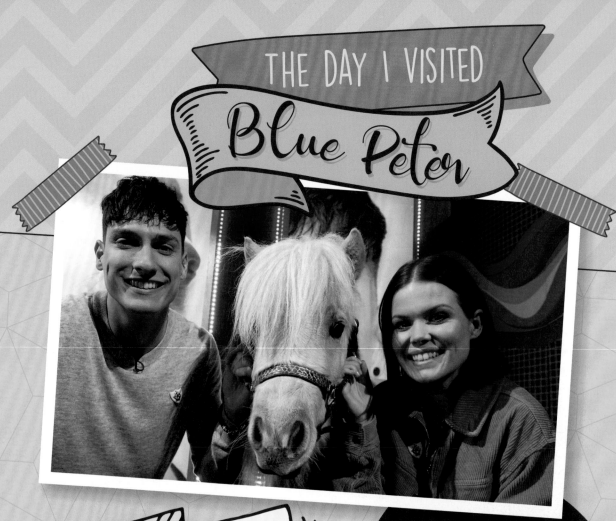

THE GREEN ROOM

Our lorry parked in the loading bay all day, which was just next to the studio. I jumped out and then we went to the green room that I waited in with my hooman and Rusty, too! It had a green carpet and I thought it was grass.

"I WAS AN ABSOLUTE STAR — MUCH BETTER BEHAVED THAN THE BLUE PETER DOG HENRY, APPARENTLY, WHO ALWAYS BARKS!"

The studio was quite big with separate areas – one with the Blue Peter sofas, a stage set up for the band to play and an area for me. The lights were bright and there were lots of people doing different jobs. Alice wore a microphone and during the practices the team upstairs were watching and giving feedback via earpieces!

After the practice, we had a mini photoshoot while everyone else then ran through their bits.

PRACTICE MAKES PERFECT

We arrived at 10am and went straight into morning rehearsals. The show is live, but we practiced everything at least twice so that we knew what was happening.

RUSTY CAME, TOO!

Rusty was only about 12 weeks old at the time so was very small. He got passed around from person to person. He even slept in Lindsey's lap while she had her make-up done and the Blossoms band wanted to steal him! Then, Alice got her make-up done – which everyone had so they didn't look like a ghost in front of the camera!

" JUST BEFORE LUNCH I WAS ON BBC NEWSROUND, TOO. THEY DID THE FILMING IN THE BLUE PETER STUDIO. "

READY, STEADY, LIVE...

Just before we went live, the children arrived (the live audience) and we had one more run-through with them. They were from a local school and they were all very excited to see a pony in the studio. There were lots of loud sounds, lights, cameras at lots of different angles and people. I loved the attention and everyone kept saying how good I was! It was the first time I've heard a band live.

" I DIDN'T HAVE ANY SNACKS BECAUSE THEY DISTRACT ME WHEN I'M WORKING. BUT I HAD PLENTY WHEN WE GOT HOME! "

I ♥ BLOSSOMS

SMALL BUT Mighty

TRY THESE fun-sized puzzles!

TINY BASIC

Look for each word in the letter trail and tick them off as you find them

k s m u i l l m i n i a t u r e a a
r c i m e y l o E r u m i t i n y a n
o t u r l y c l i t t l e t e e n y
u e s m a l l f i e l k e r c j

Small ⬤ Tiny ⬤ Little ⬤ Teeny ⬤ Micro ⬤ Miniature ⬤

TRAIL BLAZER

Nothing gets in the way of this pony and his snax!

CAN YOU HELP TEDDY GET TO HIS TREATS?

'BOOM'

'BOOM'

A
B
C

SNEAKY PEEK

Can you spot the four differences between these two shots?

A

B

THE ONE AND ONLY!

Which of these Shetlands is the real Teddy?

A

B

C

D

E

Find the answers on page 84.

MEET AND GREET

EVERYONE LOVES RUSTY…!

All about baby bro

Name: Rusty
Age: One
Breed: Working Cocker Spaniel
Family: Rocky and Chip are his canine companions and he shares hoomans Alice and Molly with me. But he really loves yours truly, his big bro, best of all! Won't leave me alone...
Loves: Pats and cuddles, swimming beside me, licking my snout and hitching a ride on me!
Dislikes: Baths – especially with girly-scented shampoo – and big, loud barky bois.

Heart melt alert

When he's snoozing do you think he's dreaming of huge adventures?

Catching up with me

He may have started out tiny but he has grown sooo much!

Rusty's happy place

My lil champ has to look flawless if he's going to appear on the 'gram with me, I do have standards, you know!

BESTIES ALWAYS WITH THIS DUDE

Double act

Best friends FOREVER!

NOW YOU *see me...*

FOOTBALL SKILLZ
It's only a matter of time before I get the call from Gareth Southgate...

GO TEAM GB!

ELITE ATHLETE
Olympics here I come

INCOGNITO
This is my go-to outfit when I need to pop to the shops. I've so nailed the off-duty look!

STRIPES
Is a zebra black with white stripes, or white with black stripes?

30

#SANDOWN

COWMOOFLAGE
Enough said!

HELLOOO, DAAARLING!
Ladies day is a must for a gent like me.

DAY AT THE RACES
When I need to blend in with da grown ups at the races.

TEDDY'S TIPS

How to rock your best undercover look:

1 Do your research so that you don't make any rookie style errors. Policeman's hat at Ascot is a no, no!

2 Beg, borrow, steal from a hooman whatever you need for your outfit.

3 Be brave, be bold – if the occasion calls for it, obvs!

ON-TREND

Five a day

TEDDY MAKES

You will need:

- baler twine and scissors
- a selection of fruit and vegetables – carrots, parsnips, turnips and apples work well
- skewer and a sharp knife
- a grown-up helper

What not to use:

- cabbage
- broccoli
- cauliflower
- rhubarb
- onion
- potatoes
- tomatoes
- acorns

What to do:

1. With your grown-up helper, cut the fruits and veggies up so they're the right size for nibbling.

2. Use the skewer to poke holes through the middle of the veg, keeping the sharp point facing away from you.

3. Knot one end of the twine, then thread the other end through the holes so the fruit and veg pieces are stacked on top of each other.

4. Ask your grown-up to hang your kebab somewhere safe for your pony to nibble on it.

FILLING MY TUM!

DAY TIME IS *playtime!*

WE COULD BE TWINS

07:00

I love to start the day with breakfast in bed – it's my favourite snack of the day.

07:30

After breakfast, Rusty's allowed in to say hello and maybe even lead me to my field. Not that I need any help, as I know exactly where I'm heading.

08:00

After a few laps of the field with da boys it's time to settle down and have a lovely, long nibble of the grass.

12:00

Even a superstar like me needs to earn his keep. Today I'm off to one of the regular hospices I visit, where I'm paid handsomely in hugs and kissez for my effort.

34

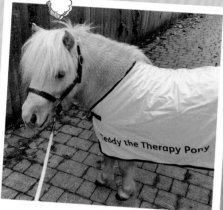

HUGS AND KISSEZ

WORKING 9–5

16:00

When I get back from a hard day at the office, I like to let my floof down and go for a swim in the Thames – in the summer anyway! Turns out I'm a fair-weather floofer and apparently, I'm not allowed in the jacuzzi – but I'm working on it!

17:00

Time for a snack attack! I like to have a handful of *Safe & Sound* fibre-based feed and a small sprinkling of treats, washed down with a dash of water to round off my day.

18:00

Lights out and time to say goodnight to my baby bro. Night, night!

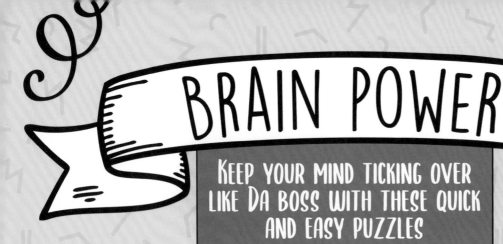

BRAIN POWER

Keep your mind ticking over like Da boss with these quick and easy puzzles

TRUE OR FALSE?

Which of these is not a true fact about Teddy?

A He loves Snax ☐

B His owner is called Alison ☐

C He is a therapy pony ☐

D He is 78cm tall ☐

E He is an international heartbreaker ☐

UP CLOSE AND PEROSNAL

Work out which of these cropped pictures are Teddy and his m8tes!

A

B

C

D

E

.... Teddy

.... Rusty

.... Finley

.... Doris

.... Podge

Find the answers on page 84.

SAY WHAAAT?!

Write your funniest caption for Teddy here

#ORIGINAL

....

SNACK ALERT

Can you find all the treats that Ponies of all shapes and sizes love in this wordsearch?

```
M  T  I  S  S  J  O  U  S  B  A  D  L  P
N  I  Q  P  O  I  T  E  M  M  O  G  O  F
C  J  N  U  C  A  R  R  O  T  S  L  M  W
Y  J  N  T  M  K  E  J  A  O  O  P  P  I
G  A  S  A  X  W  R  C  N  S  Y  A  U  P
O  P  U  T  E  E  S  W  Q  D  G  R  M  J
B  P  R  D  K  N  A  M  Y  O  I  S  P  K
R  L  E  V  H  L  L  N  R  A  S  N  K  S
E  E  P  H  C  E  L  E  R  Y  C  I  I  F
A  S  T  R  D  D  Y  B  N  E  R  P  N  C
W  R  N  O  E  K  D  U  O  I  Y  N  E  V
Y  S  A  E  P  P  A  N  S  R  A  G  U  S
U  A  R  Y  T  R  O  P  E  N  C  Y  C  T
X  A  S  U  G  M  M  O  H  G  R  T  S  A
```

WHY'S AN ICE LOLLY NOT ON THIS LIST??

- [ ] APPLES
- [ ] CARROTS
- [ ] POLOS
- [ ] CELERY
- [ ] PUMPKIN
- [ ] SUGAR SNAP PEAS
- [ ] MINT
- [ ] PARSNIP

WHEN PODGE MET Teddy and Rusty

TEDDY

ALICE

RUSTY

PODGE

39

MEET AND GREET

DORIS AND ME GO WAAAY BACK

SHE IS MY NOW AND FOREVER...

I FIRST MET DORIS ON JULY 7 2016

All about Doris

Name: Doris
AKA: Dorisbear
Colour: Chestnut
Breed: Miniature Shetland Pony
BFF: The one and only Willberry Wonder Pony
Loves: Kicking cancer's butt. Coming inside. Hanging out with Teddy the Shetland. Jumping. Snax of the sweetest vegetable kind. But most importantly, Doris loves making Willberry Wishes come true!
Dislikes: Being too busy to spend quality time with her boyfriend and best pal.
Find Doris on insta @doris_the_shetland

Doris' day job

Doris loves doing good deedz. She's all about Hannah's Willberry Wonder Pony Charity.

Side by side

Ponies that munch together, stay together. Doris loves tasty grass and is happy to share a hay snack, but her favourite treat is carrot and she keeps those all to herself.

LITTLE LEGS

This is when we walked alongside the big boys doin' important police business.

Date night

We love nothing more than a spot of quality time together – it's so important when you're both super-busy... This is one of our go-to places. Check out our favourite doorman's smile, he's always sooo pleased to see us. Doesn't my floof look good in this shot?! Oh and Doris looks mighty fine, too.

TOTALLY TALLER THAN THESE DAFFODILS!
TEDDY THE SHETLAND
crazy hair, don't care

STEP-BY-STEP GUIDE TO
maintaining the floof

YOU MIGHT THINK I ROLL OUT OF BED EACH MORNING LOOKING THIS GOOD, BUT IT ACTUALLY TAKES A FAIR BIT OF GROOMING TO KEEP THE FLOOF THIS VOLUMIZED!

you'll need
- a hooman
- plastic or rubber curry comb
- body brush
- hoof pick
- detangler
- mane comb
- hoof polish or conditioner

1 Start by picking out my hooves. Use the pick from heel to toe to make sure there are no stones or debris making me uncomfortable. See page 70 for my full foot-care manual.

2 Now it's time to tackle the mud. Alice says I'm her favourite because I don't like wallowing in mud, which means this part will take no time at all! With a plastic or rubber curry comb on my bod, use a circular motion to remove any dried-on mud. Even though I'm always pretty clean, I really enjoy this part of my pamper sesh – it's just like a massage.

3 Next you'll need a dandy brush. I like the ones with long bristles the most for flicking the dust and dirt away. Work from top to tail, brushing in the direction of my coat.

4 Next comes my face and legs. Bin off the curry comb and dandy brush in favour of something nice and soft like a body brush – I'm a sensitive modern man after all! Brush me in the direction of my coat and be particularly careful around my eyes.

5 You can give me a quick polish with the body brush all over, too, to make me shine bright like a diamond. Skip this step when I'm living out without a rug, as it can strip away the natural oils which make my coat waterproof.

6 Now for the floof. Give my mane and tail a quick spray with de-tangler to help get the knots out, then gently comb through with a wide-toothed comb until all the tangles have gone.

7 Finally, you can paint some hoof polish or conditioner onto my little trotters for some extra pizzazz!

How do I look?

47

#INTERNATIONAL

HEARTBREAKER

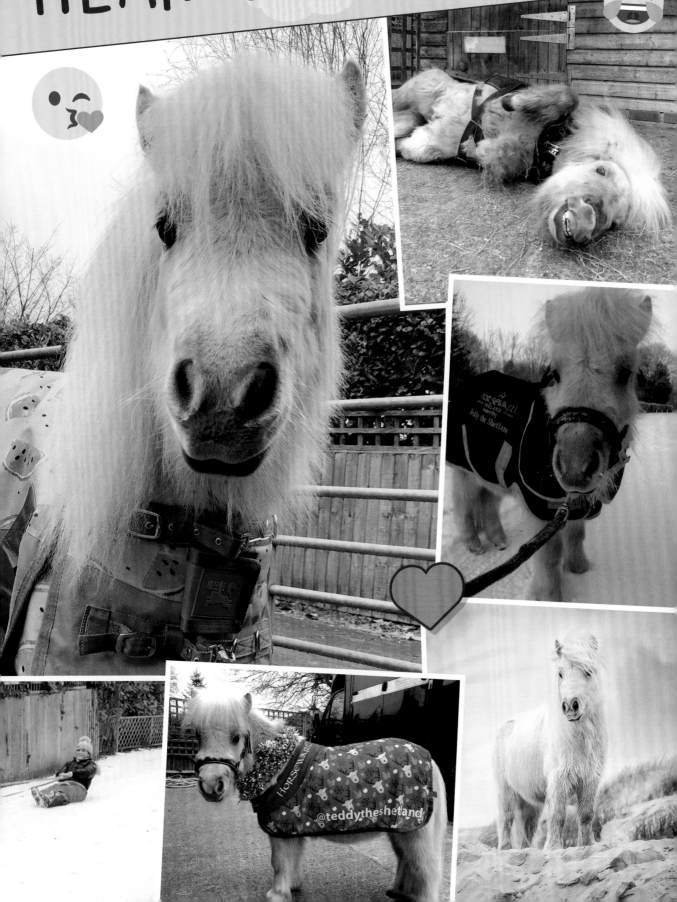

@teddytheshetland

Picnic
WITH THE FAM

Alright, who switched the sugar and salt around? Move back two squares.

One cup of tea later and my energy levels are through the roof! Take another turn.

TEDDY

Molly's stepped in to help butter bread for sandwiches! Move forward two squares.

Whoops, forgot to preheat the oven! Move back three squares.

Hang on, I'm just uploading a post to the 'gram! Miss a go.

TEDDY THE SHETLAND

Here's one I made earlier! Take another turn.

START

50

TAKE ME TO THE BEACH

Bringing my international heartbreaker style to the seaside

TEDDY'S TIPS

Have fun in the sun

Woolly adventurers like me still need protecting from the hot sun. Cover your pony's sensitive spots with sunscreen. Remind us to drink too, so that we keep our gorgeous bods in tip-top condition.

My best angle

When you take your pony to the beach, have your phone or camera charged. We all look so good with the waves behind us and the wind in our floof!

Vitamin sea

Dis Shetland needs his regular dose of the good stuff. Letting your pony splash around in the water will make him sooo happy. Plzthankx

A hard-working superstar needs his downtime

CHILLAXIN'

"LOVIN' THE WINDSWEPT LOOK"

53

TEDDY MAKES

Cake time

You will need:

For the sponge cake
- 350g softened butter
- 350g caster sugar
- 6 medium eggs (lightly beaten)
- 2 teaspoons vanilla extract
- 350g self-raising flour
- 2 teaspoons baking powder

For the buttercream
- 400g softened butter
- 1kg icing sugar
- 4 teaspoons vanilla extract
- 4 tablespoons milk

For the decoration
- black, brown and cream coloured sugar pastes
- brown food colouring to colour the buttercream

Equipment
- 2 x 20cm round cake tins – bases lined with baking paper
- large mixing bowl
- sieve
- electric or hand whisk
- wire cooling rack
- wooden spoon
- spatula
- palette knife and long sharp knife
- 25cm round cake board
- rolling pin
- large piping bag
- rosette piping tubes

What to do:

1 Ask your grown-up to help you make your sponge cake. Start by preheating the oven to 180°C (350°F, gas 4). Pop the butter, sugar, eggs and vanilla extract into the mixing bowl and sift over the flour and baking powder. Using the whisk, beat all of the ingredients together into a mighty thick batter.

2 Split the mixture between the two tins, then bake in the centre of the oven for 45–60 mins, or until the cake's risen and is firm to the touch. Leave the cakes to cool for a few minutes – absolutely no scoffing – and then turn out onto the wire rack to cool.

3 Make the buttercream filling by placing the butter, icing sugar, vanilla extract, milk and a drop of brown food colouring into a large mixing bowl. Beat together with a wooden spoon or electric mixer unit until smooth and creamy.

4 When the sponges are cool as a cucumber, ask your grown-up to use a long sharp knife to cut both cakes in half horizontally so you have a top and bottom. Spread a layer of buttercream on one half, place it on the cake board and pop another layer of sponge on top. Repeat until you have four layers with butttercream in between each one. Don't be stingy, but leave plenty for decorating!

For the decoration:

1 Using a palette knife, slap a layer of buttercream over the sides and top of your cake.

2 Dust the worktop with icing sugar and roll out the cream sugar paste. Lay this over the cake and carefully smooth it out over the top and sides.

3 Make some ears with the cream sugar paste and a little bit of the brown in the centre, then place on top of the cake. Create my snout using the brown sugar paste and make my eyes using the black. Position them on the front of the cake.

4 Place the buttercream into the piping bag and create da floof by piping rosettes of buttercream onto the cake.

DA FLOOF
It's up to you how floofy you make me, but the more the merrier imo. To pipe, fill the piping bag, twist the top, hold the bag upright, and squeezing tightly press down to release the buttercream. Swirl or blob as you like. Repeat all over the top of the cake and down the sides, refilling the bag as you go.

GO—FASTER floofers!

The big thrill of the Grand National for little Shetlands like me

LET'S GO!

THERE'S NO STOPPING US!

The Shetland Pony Grand National gives Shetlands and their jockeys the chance to race over small steeplechase fences – having a total blast and raising money for charity at the same time. 10 combinations line up to take part in each race and the winners can qualify for a super-spangly final at the London Olympia Horse show.

The ponies draw the order in which they start, and the race begins with the ponies in walk as they are counted down to the start. It would be great if we could all line up in one straight line, but we just get too excited. You have to gallop round the course as fast as you can, jumping all of the fences. Be careful! If your hooman falls off during the race, you are automatically disqualified.

Floofy fact

Ponies who are aged 17 or over must have a letter signed by their doctor to say they are fit to race.

Floofy fact

Hoomans must be aged between 9 and 14 years old to enter the Olympia qualifying races.

Floofy fact

Floofers must be between 9.1hh and 10.2hh (around 94-107cm) so that's me out! They also need to be aged 5-20 years and be registered with the Shetland Pony Stud Book Society

THE HOOMAN DRESS CODE

- White racing breeches
- Racing boots with a raised heel of a minimum 1cm thickness (no rubber boots or jodhpur boots and chaps)
- Body protector and safety hat tested to the current British safety standards
- Racing silks – the spangly tops real jockeys wear
- No jewellery or make up
- No whips or spurs

THE FLOOFERS DRESS CODE

- A black or brown bridle with any bit (apart from driving bits)
- Optional martingales
- Saddle with an over girth and safety stirrups
- Numbered saddle cloths
- Go-faster stripes – just kidding!

WORK IT

 STAY FIT LIKE DA BOSS!

When you wish you didn't have a long name...

Teddy the Shetland!!!!

What you need to do:

Spell out your name to create your own workout, so if you have the letter T do 10 squats and for E it's 10 press ups. Do this every day and you'll soon be Olympic athlete-worthy, like me.

A = Bend down and touch your toes 5 times

B = 20 bunny hops

C = 20 arm circles

D = Squat low like a frog and hold for 30 seconds

E = 10 press ups

F = 30 second wall sit

G = Gallop around the room for 1 minute lifting your knees as high as you can

H = 10 burpees

I = Hold a plank for 20 seconds

J = Jump up and down 10 times, crouching low as you land

K = 20 knee lifts

L = 5 lunges

M = Lie on the floor and stretch out as far as you can, count to 50

N = Rotate your arms in each direction for 30 seconds

O = Run on the spot for 45 seconds

P = 20 sit ups

Q = 10 reverse crunches

R = Skip for 2 minutes

S = 15 star jumps

T = 10 squats

U = Swing both arms to the right, then to the left 10 times each way

V = Stand tall for 30 seconds with one leg tucked up

W = Hop on each leg 10 times

X = Try a reverse lunge 5 times

Y = Sprint backwards and forwards between two chairs 20 times

Z = Hold a side plank for 20 seconds

TEDDY'S TIPS

If you do an exercise that focuses on one leg or side, do the other one the next day for perfect alignment.

YOUR WORKOUT

Letter	Exercise
....	....
....	....
....	....
....	....
....	....
....	....
....	....
....	....
....	....
....	....
....	....
....	....
....	....
....	....
....	....
....	....
....	....
....	....
....	....
....	....

PONY FIT

THREE QUICK EXERCISES TO KEEP US ON OUR TOES

1

Take your fave pony out to do some running and stopping exercises – run a little bit longer than the time before each time, and stop more often.

2

Teach us to jump! We will love to show off our skillz and if you start off with a low jump you can then build it up as your pony gets more confident.

3

On a lead, walk your pony forward a few steps, then back it up the same number of steps.

TEDDY'S TIPS

Make it fun and you'll keep our attention for longer. And reward us with healthy snax – lots of snax!

DA STABLE TOUR

SMALL AND PERFECTLY FORMED, JUST LIKE ME!

I have a window here for when I want some fresh air.

These hanging snax look so tasty. Maybe if I stand on tip toes I could try one?

My stable door is in three parts, otherwise I would not be able to see out!

Behind here is where my hooman ties me to groom me. I am not a fan of grooming...

I HAVE MY OWN GARDEN, TOO

TEDDY'S TIP

When we have a sleepover, Podge sleeps in with me. But every pony needs his space so we have the door open and we can come and go. The horsebox is next to my stable with the ramp open so we can nip in there if we need to!

My kit is kept in here. If Podge starts snoring he'll be in there, too!

This is where my hay's hiding. Out of sight, and out of mind...

61

TEDDY THE SHETLAND in Rad New Pad

A STAR LIKE ME DESERVES A PALACE TO MATCH!

THIS IS MORE LIKE IT. THE KING HAS FOUND HIS CASTLE, AND ALL IS RIGHT IN THE WORLD.

TEDDY! WHERE ARE YOU? IF I WERE A PAMPERED PONY, WHERE WOULD I HIDE?

I WONDER WHAT THE OTHERS ARE UP TO. MAYBE PARADISE FOR ONE ISN'T PARADISE AFTER ALL...

WHO NEEDS A MODERN BACHELOR PAD? HOME IS DEFINITELY WHERE THE PALS ARE.

THERE YOU ARE! HAVE YOU BEEN LOOKING FOR DREAM HOMES AGAIN?

THERE SHE IS, ACT NATURAL!

THE END

HANNAH'S WILLBERRY WONDER PONY

HANNAH'S WILLBERRY
WONDER PONY
#KICKINGCANCERSBUTT

BRINGING JOY WHEN LIFE IS REALLY TOUGH

Hannah's Willberry Wonder Pony is a charity set up by a young talented rider Hannah Francis. She was very poorly with a rare form of cancer, after a courageous fight she sadly died at 18 years old. Hannah's charity continues to fund research and grant Willberry's Wishes.

Who is Willberry?

He's a petite brunette who's a little over one hand tall. He was Hannah's fave cuddly toy and has the very important job of continuing the work of Hannah's Charity. You might see other Berry ponies out and about that look just like Willberry – but he's the only one with a red scarf.

What do they do?

Hannah said when she rode a horse it made her feel normal again. She wanted to help other seriously ill people by giving them an equine experience to remember. A wish from Willberry could be anything from a VIP day at a horsey event to meeting a favourite equestrian personality – like me! The charity visits events, runs super-fun challenges and you can even help by taking home your very own Berry pony, too.

Life as a mascot

I became a Willberry mascot way back in 2016 – when I also met fellow Willberry mascot and love of my life, Doris. It's a serious job and sees me attending many publicity photoshoots and events. Here's one where Doris and I got to eat really posh grass right by Horse Guards Parade!

On the draw

PENS AT THE READY? WHY NOT DRAW YOUR OWN TRIBUTE TO INTERNATIONAL HEARTBREAKER TEDDY, FOLLOWING THIS EASY STEP-BY-STEP GUIDE

Step 1

Draw a circle for Teddy's head and two for his body, then add ears and his nose.

Step 2

Get the head shape as you want it before you move on, this is the essence of Teddy.

Step 3

A Shetland's body is very distinctive – with a low-level belly and broad back.

Step 4

Legs come next. Front ones first. Don't make them too long, sorry Teddy!

Step 5

Now's the time for da floof. Go as big and as floofy as you dare!

Step 6

Finish off with the tail and any distinctive markings you've spotted. Now add colour.

Teddy's teasers

SPOT THE DIFFERENCE

Can you spot six differences between these two pictures?

YAY OR NEIGH

See if you can work out if Teddy is telling the truth (yay) or a lie (neigh)!

1 I LOVE SWIMMING IN THE THAMES
YAY ☐ NEIGH ☐

2 WHEN I GROW UP I WANT TO BE AN EVENTER JUST LIKE FINLEY
YAY ☐ NEIGH ☐

3 I ONCE MET ACTUAL VALEGRO
YAY ☐ NEIGH ☐

MAY THE HORSE BE WITH YOU

4 I STARRED IN AN EPISODE OF STAR WARS
YAY ☐ NEIGH ☐

WORDSEARCH

Can you find all these words? Tick them off when you find them.

```
R U S Y T E A T I D R A U N
P I Y N O P Y P A R E H T D
A O J A K L I Z M E B R C M
D A D A P N E T Y S A O S T
N X A G D A F D O R E S I T
L A O O E A D H C S U L R C
B N R O W E N G U I S C O A
A S C D T N A S E K A N D S
S T E T R A B I G E D I T A
M A T M F L O O F A T C I T
D R O V J U G L A M A L P H
P A C R Y N O M A Y T R O A
A E R C M E M E R M A L B U
T F L T L M T A Y T S U R A
```

☐ RUSTY
☐ PODGE
☐ DORIS
☐ SNAX
☐ FLOOF
☐ THERAPY PONY
☐ TEDDY

69

ALL ABOUT hooves

Whether you're big or you're small, every floofer needs four healthy hooves to be happy. Here's my guide to keeping my little twinkle toes in tip-top condition!

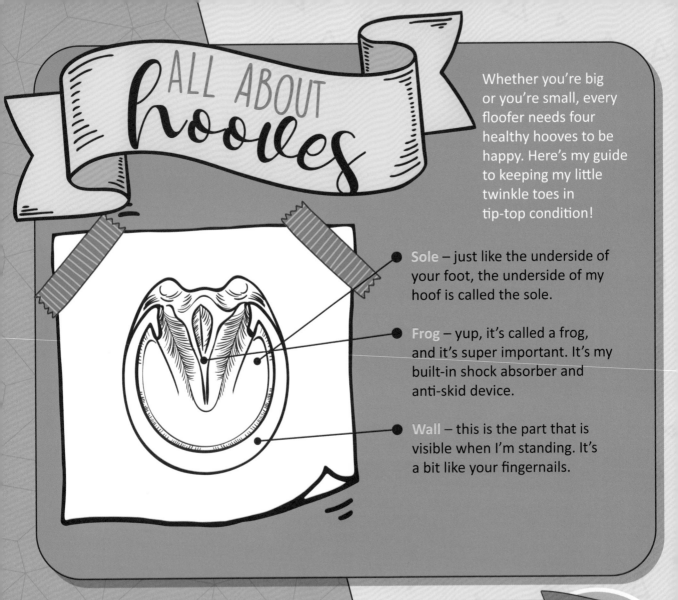

Sole – just like the underside of your foot, the underside of my hoof is called the sole.

Frog – yup, it's called a frog, and it's super important. It's my built-in shock absorber and anti-skid device.

Wall – this is the part that is visible when I'm standing. It's a bit like your fingernails.

SPOTLESS HOOVES

If I've learned one thing, it's that you need super-clean hooves if you're going to go waltzing into a hooman's home anytime soon.

Here's how to do it properly:
• Slide your hand down the inside of the pony's leg, and gently lift his hoof off the ground.
• Supporting the hoof with the hand closest to the pony, use a hoof pick in your other hand to remove dirt and stones.
• Always work from the pony's heel to toe so that if your hoof pick slips you won't damage any of the sensitive areas of the hoof.
• Using the brush on the back of the hoof pick, gently brush away any remaining mud.
• Lower the hoof back to the ground.
• Repeat for all four hooves.

NEW SHOES ANYONE?

Lots of horses and ponies have metal horseshoes fitted by their farrier, but as I don't do lots of hard work (Shhh! Don't tell anyone I admitted that!) I just have a trim every 6-8 weeks. It might look painful as the farrier trims and files my hooves, but really, it's just like having your nails done!

FLOOFY FACT

On the rare occasions I do lots of walking on hard ground, I wear my sparkly hoof boots so that I don't wear out my hooves.

FLOOFY FACT

In the wild, ponies roam many miles a day, which naturally wears down their hooves so they don't need to see the farrier.

FLOOFY FACT

Some hoomans oil their pony's hooves to make them super-shiny for the show ring. I prefer a hoof conditioner on mine, which helps to keep them healthy, as well as looking da business.

71

TEDDY THE SHETLAND

crazy hair, don't care

Hobby HORSE

Ho! Ho! Ho!

1 Help Santa on Christmas Eve.

Why should Rudolph get all the attention?

2 Land a speaking role in a period drama.

As Lady Crawley said, "Never complain, never explain."

3 Watch this dude grow tall.

Me and Rusty are besties for life. Enough said!

There's a whole lotta world out there to discover

4 Travel more.

So many people to see
#MakingMemories

5 Help out wherever and whoever I can.

As Taylor Swift once said, "You can't spell awesome without me!"

A SHETLAND WITH HOBBIES IS ONE HAPPY PONY!

6 Spend more time with this special hooman.

Is she stealing my style?

LOOK MUM, I'M ON TV!

7 Become a TV star!

After Blue Peter... the sky's the limit!

8 Enjoy a snow day.

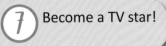

Check out my clips on da social - skillz man!

Taming the FLOOF!

LOOKING THIS GOOD TAKES WORK, YOU KNOW!

HOW TO: COPY MY STYLE

What to do:

1 Grab a mane comb, some plaiting or hair bands and your fave floofer – it's time to get Insta-ready!

2 Brush through the mane until it's smooth and knot-free. You're looking to achieve the ultimate silky floof.

3 You don't need to plait the whole mane. Pick a few sections and plait to the bottom, then use a band to secure.

4 Thread some delicate flowers through the plaits for extra pizzazz! Hey presto, I'm festival ready!

HOW TO: PLAIT A TAIL

What to do:

1 Take two strands from the left and one from the right and start plaiting. As the first section comes back over the top of the plait, combine another small section of hair with it.

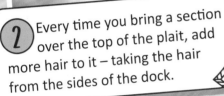

2 Every time you bring a section over the top of the plait, add more hair to it – taking the hair from the sides of the dock.

3 Once your plait reaches three quarters of the way down your pony's dock, stop adding hair and plait it straight down.

4 When your plait reaches the bottom of the tail, tuck it up and under itself before securing with a band.

TEDDY'S TIP

My hooman uses detangler spray to on my mane and tail to help keep da floof shiny and knot-free. It makes brushing it a piece of cake, too.

77

Pony PUMPKIN

TEDDY MAKES

THIS NO-CARVE PUMPKIN MIGHT NOT BE THE SCARIEST – BUT IT'S CERTAINLY THE FLOOFIEST!

You will need:

- pumpkin
- acrylic paint
- paintbrush
- scissors
- glue
- template on page 85
- feather boa

1. Paint the whole of your pumpkin with the acrylic paint. Make sure you put paper down first to protect any surfaces.

2. Leave your pumpkin to dry – this could take up to 24 hours.

- 24h -

3. Cut out the template on page 85 or trace it onto some paper and then cut around the eyes, ears, mouth and forelock.

4. Glue the features to your pumpkin to make it look just like Teddy.

5. Add some extra floof by draping a feather boa over your pumpkin.

"APPLE BOBBING IS MY FAVOURITE HALLOWEEN GAME — I'M ALL ABOUT THE SNAX"

HOW WELL DO YOU KNOW TEDDY?

TRY THIS FUN-SIZED QUIZ TO FIND OUT!

1 TEDDY RUNS AS FAST AS A:

A Llama ☐
B Lightning bolt ☐
C Unicorn ☐

2 WHAT IS TEDDY'S HOOMAN CALLED?

A Alice ☐
B Rusty ☐
C Sandy ☐

3 WHAT YEAR WAS TEDDY BORN?

A 2015 ☐
B 2016 ☐
C 2014 ☐

4 WHERE WAS TEDDY WHEN HE MET THE HOUSEHOLD CAVALRY?

A Buckingham Palace ☐
B Olympia Horse Show ☐
C At home ☐
(they popped round for tea)

5 CAN YOU SPOT THE REAL TEDDY?

6 WHAT IS TEDDY'S FAVE HOBBY, APART FROM SNAX, OBVS?

A Modelling the latest fashions ☐
B Galloping over twiglets ☐
C Being an equine superstar ☐

HOW DID YOU DO?

7 WHAT BREED IS TEDDY'S LITTLE BRUV?

A Poodle ☐

B Miniature Dachshund ☐

C Working Cocker ☐

8 WHAT IS TEDDY MOST LIKELY TO BE THINKING IN THIS PICTURE?

A Loving da floof! ☐

B I iz not a toy! ☐

C I'm an elite athlete! ☐

Woah!
Check out these cute pictures of me. I should be a model... oh duh, I am!

Find the answers on page 85

5–8 POINTS

Woah, are you stalking me? That's amazing! You know me as well as Alice, and some. Loving the fandom. #superfan

3–5 POINTS

I can see we could be good mates, there's a whole load of love going on already. Keep up the good work! #friendship

1–3 POINTS

Hi I'm Teddy, have we met before? Either way, I'm very pleased to welcome you to the fam! Let's talk more often...

BLOOPERS

How come there always seems to be a camera around when things don't go to plan! #Professional #KeepSmiling

I think I'm stuck

Please look at the camera

Tickle time?

Look which way?

Think I'm onto something...

You can't catch me

ANSWERS AND TEMPLATES

PAGE 26 SMALL BUT MIGHTY

TINY BASIC

k s m u i l l m i n i a t u r e a a
r c i m e y l o E r u m i t i n y a n
o t u r l y c l i t t l e t e e n y
u e s m a l l f i e l k e r c j

TRAIL BLAZER

A
B
C

'BOOM'

'BOOM'

SNEAKY PEEK

THE ONE AND ONLY

C

PAGE 36 BRAIN POWER

TRUE OR FALSE

B His owner is really called Alice

UP CLOSE AND PERSONAL

E .... Teddy
A .... Rusty
C .... Finlay
D .... Doris
B .... Podge

SNACK ALERT

```
M T I S S J O U S B A D L P
N I Q P O I T E M M O G O F
C J N U C A R R O T S L M W
Y J N T M K E J A O O P P I
G A S A X W R C N S Y A U P
O P U T E E S W Q D G R M J
B P R D K N A M Y O I S P K
R L E V H L L N R A S N K S
E E P H C E L E R Y C I I F
A S T R D D Y B N E R P N C
W R N O E K D U O I Y N E V
Y S A E P P A N S R A G U S
U A R Y T R O P E N C Y C T
X A S U G M M O H G R T S A
```

PAGE 68 TEDDY'S TEASERS

SPOT THE DIFFERENCE

84

TEDDY'S TEASERS

YAY OR NEIGH

1. **YAY** – It's true, but only when it's warm
2. **NEIGH** – that looks far too much like hard work!
3. **YAY** – and I gave him some tips!
4. **NEIGH** – it was Blue Peter

WORDSEARCH

```
R U S Y T E A T I D R A U N
P I Y N O P Y P A R E H T D
A O J A K L I Z M E B R C M
D A D A P N E T Y S A O M T
N X A G D A F D O R E S I T
L A O O E A D H C S U L R C
B N R O W E N G U I S C O D
A S C D T N A S E K A N D D
S T E T R A B I G E D I T A
M A T M F L O O F A T C I T
D R O V J U G L A M A L P H
P A C R Y N O M A Y T R O A
A E R C M E M E R M A L B U
T F L T L M T A Y T S U R A
```

HOW WELL DO YOU KNOW TEDDY

1 – A   5 – C
2 – A   6 – C
3 – A   7 – C
4 – B   8 – A

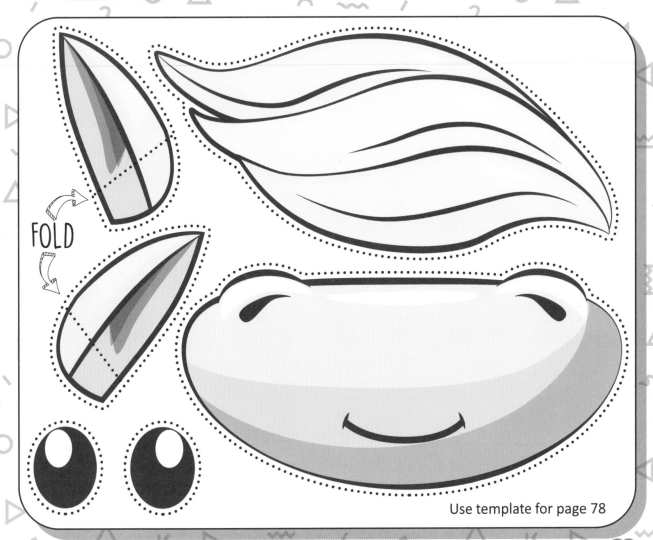

FOLD

Use template for page 78